often it is a kind of shorthand which conveys specific meanings quite precisely. Throughout this publication we will use the standard terms because it is important to become familiar with them, but we will explain what they mean as we go along, and you will find a Glossary in Section 7.

Let's start by looking at the term ICT (information and communications technology). Where 'IT' refers to using a computer for word processing, desktop publishing, or working with a spreadsheet or database, for example, ICT has an emphasis on communication – using a computer to send and receive information. This can involve sending a fax or an e-mail, or posting a message on a bulletin board, which is similar to putting up a poster on a noticeboard. It might mean communicating with another teacher in your school, or with your LEA, or even with a world-wide audience, by setting up some Web pages on the Internet so that people from around the world can read about the research you have done or services which you can offer.

The Internet in particular seems to be always in the news. It is akin to a vast computer network which links up millions of computers throughout much of the world, generally via a telephone line. It provides a mechanism for communicating with other people and for finding and communicating information, whether it is text or pictures, sound, video clips or whole software programs. Part of the Internet is known as the World Wide Web (or simply, the Web), which links information world wide by the use of keywords.

What's in it for you?

Maybe you have professional concerns as a teacher:
- Where can you find satellite pictures of the weather?
- Are there any local authority guidelines about . . . ?
- How could you find out what is in the latest White Paper on education?
- Is it possible to read that article about redundancy payments which was in the *TES* about six months ago?
- How can you find pen-pals for your pupils?

Maybe the technology will benefit you personally:
- Do you want to find out what's on at the RSC?
- Do you need to plan a trip abroad and want to find more information before you go?
- Would you like to access information about the safety of genetically modified foods or new medical treatments?
- Do you have family or friends abroad, who you would like to contact?

The Internet and other communications services can provide you with information on all of the above – and indeed, on every topic you can imagine.

The Internet

The world-wide 'network of networks' connected by telephone communication systems

World Wide Web

Just part of the Internet, a vast information service based on hypertext documents which can be read by your browser

What's in it for teachers?

As an educational resource, the Internet has four distinct advantages over most other media.

Fast access

Provided that you have the system set up in an accessible place, it can be much quicker to find teaching resources and ideas on the Internet than by making a visit to a bookshop, library or teachers' centre.

Scope

The Internet not only contains information on every topic under the sun, it contains an ever-growing volume of information on them – more than any single library could ever hold.

Up-to-date information

Much data, such as timetables, exchange rates or weather information is highly ephemeral. Text-based versions of this type of data can be found in newspapers or in documents supplied by travel companies but these are not always easy materials to work with in the classroom.

Flexibility

Unlike the telephone, e-mail does not require the user to be present at the same time as the sender. If it suits you to send messages to people at 2 am, that's fine, because the recipients can pick up and reply to those messages at any time convenient for them. The same goes for the World Wide Web – it's open for business 24 hours a day.

What do you need?

If you are going to get involved with electronic communications, you need to have reasonable access to a computer so that you can use it at a time and a place to suit you. If you are only able to use the machine for a few minutes a month, you will forget everything you have learned, become extremely frustrated and make very little progress. So, where will you find a machine and exactly what do you need?

Try looking in the following places:
- Your child's bedroom
- On your desk
- On a colleague's desk
- In the local library
- At a cyber café
- In your local college
- At an adult education centre
- In an Open Learning centre.

In principle, connection can be made with most machines, but ideally you will need a 486 (or above) multimedia computer with a minimum of 4Mb RAM and 5Mb free hard disk space. This will mean looking out for a PC, Mac, Acorn or laptop which is less than five years old – anything older, and it is unlikely to be powerful enough.

To connect your computer to any Internet on-line service via a standard (dial-up) telephone connection you will need a modem, access to a telephone socket, communications software and a subscription to an Internet service provider. If you're starting from scratch, here are some features to look for:

Modems A modem converts data from the computer into a form which can be transmitted via a telephone line. In general, the faster the operating speed of the modem, the less time it takes to interact with a service, the less time you will be on-line, and the lower will be the cost of your phone call. Modem speeds are denoted by numbers – the larger the number, the faster the modem. Hence, a modem running at 28,800 bits per second is twice as fast as one running at 14,400. The majority of modems also allow you to send faxes. Modems may be built into new computers, or you can buy a free-standing model.

Phone connections Your computer will need access to a telephone socket, and whilst it's connected to an on-line service, no one can dial in or out on that line. If you only have a single line, you ought to consider installing an additional one.

Communications software You will need this to link your computer to the on-line service via the

communications. It is a 'hands on' guide which should help complete beginners to get started with electronic communications, as well as the more experienced, to gain the full benefits of new technology.

On-line, off-line, surfing, the Information Superhighway, the World Wide Web, IT, ICT – it's a whole new language which describes the activities of a growing number of people all around the world, who are gathering information and keeping in touch with one another via their computers and a phone line.

Like all new technology, it seems daunting at first. The good news is that you don't have to learn everything at once, and indeed, you don't have to learn everything about the Internet and electronic communications at all – just about the things you need to know. After all, you can drive a car without understanding the full workings of an internal combustion engine.

With any new technology there is quite a lot of jargon to master, but it is worth making an effort because

Section 1
Getting to grips with ICT

telephone line. This is usually provided with your modem, by the Internet service provider (see below) or is built into some newer computers.

Internet software This will enable you to search, retrieve and download information from the service and is likely to include a Web browser and an e-mail program. Again, this is usually provided by your Internet service provider.

Subscription to an ISP Finally, you need to have a subscription with an Internet service provider (ISP), who may be a commercial organisation, your LEA or even a local university.

Alternatively, it is possible to connect up using an ISDN telephone connection and also through the school's network of computers. Note that in addition to the costs above, you will have to pay standard telephone call charges for the time you are on-line, but virtually all ISPs offer a local connection rate, wherever they may be located.

Additional technical considerations If you are just about to buy a computer, it is worth looking for one with a built-in modem which comes with all the relevant software installed. If you are updating an existing machine by adding a modem, there are two types to choose from: internal and external. An

internal modem fits into one of the slots inside the computer whereas an external modem plugs into the computer's serial port and is about the size of a small paperback book. A modem running at 57,600 bits per second is now considered to be standard.

If you do not want to take your computer apart to add a modem, or you have a laptop computer which does not have internal expansion slots, then an external modem would be the right choice. Should you wish to be able to use a telephone on the same line as the modem but without having to change over the plugs, you will need a double connector – but remember, you will not be able to use them both at the same time.

Choosing an Internet service provider

One of the hardest decisions to make is the choice of an Internet service provider (ISP). Much is written in computer magazines that can provide help in making that choice, and a number of sources are listed in the Sources of Further Help section.

Most ISPs are large commercial organisations which charge to send information across the networks of computers that make up the Internet.

Bits and Kilobits

A bit is the smallest unit of computer information; modem speeds are measured in kbps (kilobits per second)

Browsers

Programs such as Netscape and Internet Explorer, which convert Web-based documents from HTML (Hypertext Mark-up Language) so your computer can display it

They will typically offer you access to a gateway to the Internet, access to Usenet newsgroups (a vast collection of bulletin boards) and your own e-mail address. Increasingly, however, other non-commercial organisations are offering services as ISPs and, as the National Grid for Learning develops, LEAs are likely to provide a wide range of communications services.

There is a wide range of service providers already and a useful way of finding a reliable one is to ask friends, other schools, your LEA ICT Centre or Schools' Library Service, who may also be able to offer you trial access. Otherwise, check the computer magazines and try out their free software to see if it gives you the facilities you want at a suitable price.

There are basically two types of access via an ISP: unfiltered and filtered. Unfiltered services give you access to the entire contents of the Internet, including those sites and newsgroups which may contain dubious or offensive material. Conversely, filtered services block access to known offensive sites and newsgroups, although it must be remembered that no system can guarantee that a user will not access unsuitable material. Several ISPs offer both types of services.

The majority of ISPs charge a monthly or annual amount for unlimited access to the Internet. A few providers also charge an hourly use rate. Virtually all providers offer local telephone call rates so that it costs the same to send a message to someone in your own town as to someone in Australia, because you pay for the call to your ISP only.

It might also be worth finding out what your local cable company has to offer. Some give deals which include telephone charges or bundle Internet services with other facilities in very economical packages. A growing number of ISPs offer a completely free service; you pay no monthly annual fee, just the telephone charges. These companies make their profits entirely from advertising and may represent the future for ISPs.

Where are you now?

Before we go any further, spend a little time working out where you are now. How 'ICT ready' are you? Do you have the resources you need and if not, can you obtain them? Are you sufficiently motivated to get started, and where can you obtain support if you need it? The checklist opposite should help you to establish your starting point.

Progress Checklist

Resources	Yes	No
• I have decision-making control of my budget	☐	☐
• I have access to additional budgets for involvement in a new project	☐	☐
• I have access to a computer suitable for connecting to the Internet	☐	☐
• I have access to a modem	☐	☐
• I have access to Internet software	☐	☐
• I have at least shared access to a telephone line	☐	☐
• I already have access to the Internet via school/home	☐	☐
• The school will have Internet access very soon	☐	☐

Motivation	Yes	No
• I want to set ICT as a priority for development	☐	☐
• I want to invest time now in learning about ICT	☐	☐
• I feel ICT has potential for professional development	☐	☐
• I feel ICT has potential for networking with colleagues	☐	☐
• I am keen to learn how to use electronic mail	☐	☐
• I am a confident user of electronic mail	☐	☐
• I am keen to learn how to browse the World Wide Web	☐	☐
• I am confident browsing the World Wide Web	☐	☐

Support	Yes	No
• I have a good working relationship with the IT co-ordinator in my school	☐	☐
• I have access to technical support from colleagues in school	☐	☐
• I have access to technical support at the local IT centre	☐	☐
• I have access to technical support from my Internet service provider	☐	☐
• I am sure other teachers in the local area are interested in working together	☐	☐
• Our local LEA support team is interested in using ICT to keep in contact	☐	☐

The tool for the job

If your hardware or software are more than five years old, not only will they probably be unable to support e-mail and the Internet, they may also not be Year 2000 compliant. But don't throw them away – they can still be used for word processing and other activities.

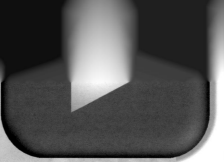

which electronic communications can bring. Enough of the theory, however: now it's time to put some of it into practice. If you have the technical equipment already and have been meaning to take the plunge for months, now really is the time to get started, with the practical activity below.

Find five people who you know use e-mail, get their addresses and keep them on a piece of paper next to the computer. Promise to write to them – guilt is a great motivator! (Note that you must write down the addresses exactly as given, with the same capitals/lower case etc. and there should never be any spaces.)

Tackling the computer

If you have not already done so, you will need to install the relevant software and enter information concerning your computer set-up and the service provider. Although installation instructions are generally clear, this can be a daunting prospect if you

Section 2
Getting started with e-mail

are not fairly confident with computers, and you could seek help from family, friends or neighbours, colleagues or your IT adviser amongst others. Another useful source of help is your service provider, so make a note of their helpline number. If possible, telephone them while sitting at the computer so that you can try out their suggestions at the time. They should know exactly how to configure the hardware and software to make connection, and there's no need to feel embarrassed about asking for help.

Once all the appropriate software and hardware is installed, you will have to re-start the computer, so follow the instructions on the computer screen.

What can you do once you're connected?

With a subscription to an Internet service provider and a fax/modem, you can send electronic messages and faxes. We will not be covering the use of faxes (refer to the manual that comes with your modem for details of this) but will cover e-mails below and information retrieval in a later section.

E-mail enables anyone with an e-mail address to communicate with any other e-mail address, even to send the same message to many addresses simultaneously, which is rather like 20 postmen

delivering the same message to 20 addresses simultaneously, and doing so for the price of one stamp. Furthermore, e-mail is faster than a letter and less intrusive than a telephone call: people can pick up their e-mail at a time which suits them, which is particularly important if you are contacting someone who lives in a country in a different time zone.

Once you subscribe to an Internet service provider you will have your own e-mail address. Your e-mail name can be in many different forms. Some ISPs give you an impersonal box number, but the trend is for friendlier addresses. Typically your address will look something like this:

jdunn@abc.co.uk

which means that Jane Dunn connects to the Internet via (@) the ABC company in the UK. The majority of addresses will be in lower case, but some may contain a few capital letters; there are never any spaces. It is vitally important that an address is entered correctly or it will not reach its destination – computers aren't as helpful as postmen, unfortunately, and won't make intelligent guesses as to what you mean.

There are many communication and e-mail programs but their basic functions are very similar. However, some e-mail programs require you to log on (connect)

IP or ISP?

You can choose between the services of an Internet Provider (IP) or Internet Service Provider (ISP). With the latter, you get additional services included (a news and weather service and access to their most popular sites, for example), where as an IP just offers access to e-mail and the Internet.

to the service provider and then instruct it to search for, and collect, your mail, whilst others download your mail automatically as part of the logging-on procedure.

Finding people on the Internet

At present there is no e-mail directory. There are several directory systems which can be used, but none offers a comprehensive listing of the millions of e-mail addresses. Consequently, the easiest way of finding someone's e-mail address is to ask them. Many people now also include it on their business cards. However, if someone sends you a message, their address will be included and you can add it to your e-mail address book for future use.

Mailboxes

These are the equivalent of 'in-trays' and 'out-trays'. Generally, e-mail software comes with three as standard: 'In', 'Out' and 'Trash' (or 'Waste Basket'). New mail is delivered to the 'In' box, mail for sending is put in the 'Out' box, and deleted mail is put into 'Trash'. Your e-mail software may allow you to create additional mailboxes, which can then become the basis of a system for storing and managing your mail. You could, for example, separate private mail from school mail.

Creating an e-mail message

As a general rule, you should always write your e-mails off-line (i.e. unconnected to your service provider). This will save you money, because all the time you are connected to your service provider you are paying telephone call charges or using up free time. It will also enable you to spend time thinking about exactly what it is you wish to say.

An e-mail message box has two sections. At the top of the box is a space for the message header or title, subject of the message and the address(es) of the person or people who will receive the message. An example is shown below.

Always complete the subject line, using a short phrase capturing the spirit of your message (in the example shown, it would be more informative to say

'Resources on Tudors'). When your correspondents collect their mail, each message is summarised as a one-line entry in a mailbox and if you correspond regularly, it can become confusing unless you can identify individual messages.

The second section is the message body itself where you type your message. In theory you can send messages of any length and you can send 'attachments' such as a long word-processed file or a picture. In practice, especially until you are a confident e-mail user, it is better to put the whole message on the page rather than in a separate file. (Sending attachments is covered on page 12). Whilst e-mail is generally seen as a less formal method of communication than letter, you do need to be fairly succinct: remember that the recipients of your e-mail will have to pay telephone charges for the length of time it takes for your message to download.

You will need to be careful of what you say in an e-mail, especially if you are sending it to a mailbox at a school since other people (pupils included) may also be able to read the message. E-mail is therefore not the best form of communication for confidential or salacious information, unless you are certain that the addressee is the only person who will read it.

Sending an e-mail

Before you start sending e-mails to your five chosen friends, how about having a dry run and sending yourself a letter just to see if the technology works and that you understand the principles?

- Open up your e-mail program (but do not connect to your service provider)
- Click on the 'New message/Create New E-mail' menu or button
- Type your e-mail address in the 'Address' or 'To' box
- Type in TEST MESSAGE in the 'Subject' box
- Type a short message in the main window.

Your software may now offer you a choice between sending the message immediately ('Send now' or a similar message) or sending it later (which will put your message into your 'Out' box ready to send the next time you connect to your service provider). It may save your message automatically (in the 'Out' box or a Filing cabinet), or you may have to request it to do this. The advantage of saving messages so they can be sent later is that you can send off a whole batch of mail together, which saves on connection time. When you are ready to send your messages, you will need to connect to your service provider.

Getting connected

Open the communications software in the normal way which is, generally, by double-clicking on the icon or menu item. The opening window will contain a menu of the Internet facilities offered by your service provider. There should be a button or menu item for you to use to make the modem dial up a connection. If there is not, click on one of the Internet facilities, such as the World Wide Web, and this will make your modem dial automatically.

A box may appear asking you to supply a password as shown above, which will be given to you by your service provider. If you have an external modem, it may flash and emit squealing sounds as it starts to communicate with the service provider's computer. Once you are connected, an icon or message will tell you that you have been successful. Your window may

E-mail and snail mail

Once you have your own e-mail address, add it to your written correspondence – it's surprising how many people will respond by e-mail rather than post.

You have mail

Many ISPs will provide multiple mailboxes with your e-mail address; give each class its own address and see who they can communicate with!

have a display that begins to time how long you have been connected to the Internet. You may also receive messages saying that any e-mails you have in your 'Out' box have been sent. Once connected, you will be able to select which part of the service you wish to connect to – e-mail for example – usually, by clicking on an icon or button.

If, despite all your efforts, you do not make a connection, telephone your service provider and hardware supplier for help, rather than struggling on alone. Occasionally, you may receive a message saying your dial-up has been unsuccessful. See page 14 to find out why this may happen.

Disconnecting

To disconnect from the Internet, select the disconnect button or menu item. Note that if you merely close the window of the facility you have been using, such as e-mail, you will still be connected to the service provider. This is designed to enable you to select another facility such as the Web, for example, without having to re-dial. Always ensure that you disconnect once you have finished completely with the service, otherwise you face the possibility of running up enormous phone bills. However, in a bid to help with this problem, most communications software gives you the choice of the line being disconnected

automatically after a certain period of time. It is particularly recommended that such a facility is used, especially where pupils will also be using the service.

Receiving e-mail

E-mail is delivered to your 'In' mailbox and you can read it whilst on or off line. However, it is good practice to get used to logging on (connecting to your service provider), collecting your mail, logging off (disconnecting) and reading it off-line. This will save on telephone call charges and give you more time to consider what to do with the messages.

Replying to messages

Most programs make it easy to send a reply:
- Open the message (usually, by double-clicking on it)
- Read the message
- Click on 'Reply' or select the menu item
- Write your message in the main body of the window
- Click on 'Send' or 'Post' (to put it into your 'Out' box, ready for sending later).

The next time you connect to your service provider, the reply will be sent automatically to the person who sent the original message together with any other people who were sent copies of the original message. However, you can alter who receives your reply by deleting or adding to the 'addresses' part of the

message. Also, you can edit the original message by deleting material not relevant to your reply. For example, if a reply is providing the answers to questions, then consider placing the responses immediately after the questions, perhaps indented. For example, you might receive a message like this:

> Hi, Anne!
>
> I realised after I'd put the phone down yesterday that I'd forgotten to ask you to confirm the date, time, venue and theme of this year's NAAFE Conference. If you could let me know, I'd be grateful.
>
> Thanks, Andy McNab

A reply could take the form:

> Hello, Andy
>
> Date: June 3rd to 5th
> Time: 9.30 to 5.30, registration on the 3rd, 9.30 -11.30
> Venue: University of Central Essex
> Theme: Learning environments for the 21st century
>
> Looking forward to seeing you there!
>
> Anne

Printing a message

There will be times when you wish to print out a message:
- Open the message (usually, by double-clicking on it)

- Read the message
- Click on 'Print'
- Save' or 'Delete' the message

Deleting a message

There is usually a button for deleting a message, either when you have read it, when you have replied to it or even before you have read it. Deleted messages are sent to your 'Trash/Wastebasket' and remain there until you close the e-mail program. If you subsequently decide you wish to keep a message you have deleted, open the 'Trash' box, click on the message and you will be offered the possibility of 'moving' the message to your 'In' tray, or another mailbox.

Saving a message

Some messages have a long shelf life since they contain important information, documents or photographs. Clicking on the 'Save' or 'File' button will move the message to another part of the program, sometimes called the 'Mailroom'. The messages will stay there until you delete them.

As you become a regular e-mail user, and particularly if you join any mailing lists (see page 14), you will need to be quite ruthless in deleting messages, otherwise you will find it increasingly time consuming and frustrating to find the one you want. Furthermore,

since many e-mail programs automatically save a copy of everything you create, your 'In' box and 'Mailroom' can soon become clogged, which is not only annoying but uses up valuable disk space and, if taken to extremes, can slow down the running of the program.

Bouncing mail

Sometimes you send an e-mail and it 'bounces' back to you with a message saying that the mail system cannot deliver it. Check you have the right address and that it is entered correctly, and try sending it again.

Some systems also automatically bounce mail from people who have temporarily suspended their mail or have not connected to their mailbox for a period of time. If all else fails you will have to phone or use 'snail mail' to find out what is going on.

Now try sending a note to your five friends.

Logging off

If you're not sure whether you have disconnected from your ISP, you can easily check with an external modem: if the lights continue to flash, you're still on-line. To make double-sure, you can simply remove the cable from the telephone socket and disconnect that way.

Progress checklist

	Yes	No
• Have you seen anyone using e-mail?	☐	☐
• Can you send yourself an e-mail?	☐	☐
• Do you know how to see if you have received an e-mail?	☐	☐
• Can you reply to an e-mail?	☐	☐
• Can you save an e-mail message?	☐	☐
• Do you know how to delete an e-mail message?	☐	☐
• Can you print an e-mail message?	☐	☐
• Have you sent your five friends an e-mail?	☐	☐

Making the most of e-mail

Most e-mail software allows you to customise it according to personal preferences, and your software guide should provide specific instructions. Below are a selection of general hints and tips.

Collect your mail regularly

Develop the habit of logging on and collecting new mail regularly – once or twice a week as a minimum. In this way you will be able to make speedy responses and avoid being overloaded with messages.

Sending large files or attachments

It is good practice to keep messages short and to the point. However, there are times when a longer communication is needed and word-processed documents can be sent as an e-mail attachment or enclosure. These are files which can be 'paper-clipped' to an e-mail message and sent along with it. They can be word-processed documents, spreadsheets, programs or virtually anything else.

Your software may contain a line called 'Attachments' as part of the message heading, have an 'Attachments' or 'Enclosure' button or may have an icon of a paper-clip. To send an attachment, click on this and select the file for attaching in the normal way. Use the body of the e-mail message to describe what the attachment is and, most importantly, the software tool used to create it. Good word-processor and spreadsheet software can deal with files from other, similar tools, but it makes sense to identify the tool you used.

If recipients of your e-mails have trouble reading your attachments even though they have the appropriate software, it is often worth trying to send the attachment without any other text in the message.

That is, append the attachment in the normal way, complete the 'To:' and 'Subject:' lines but do not write anything else. Alternatively, try saving the word-processed

file as 'plain text' or 'ASCII' before you attach it.

> Attachments: c:\word\work\report.wrd
>
> Dear Bill,
>
> Attached is a copy of the INSET report. Report.wrd, written in Word for Windows version 6
>
> Regards, John

When you receive a message with an attachment, it will be denoted either within the body of the message or the heading, according to your software. Generally, you will be asked which program you want to use to open the attachment and if it was created with the same software, it will load directly into that program. If the message was created in a similar program (such as a word processor) it will still be able to open the attachment if the sender saved the file in an appropriate format, as an ASCII file. Other formats may still work, but you may lose any formatting or have additional characters appearing in the text. However, often these can be removed fairly simply in a word-processed file by using the 'Replace all' facility, and replacing the occurrences of any unwanted character with nothing.

Using an alias

An alias is an alternative to the e-mail address given to you by your Internet service provider. Typically you may be known as: bm54@netsupplier.co.uk.

However, you can choose to have a more meaningful address by using an alias, for example: MarySmith@netsupplier.co.uk. Your service provider will advise you on how to set up an alias.

Adding your signature

A 'signature' is like a compliment slip. Users design (or scan) their own signature and most software allows you to choose to have it added to messages automatically.

Some people design very ornate signatures that look smart but occupy a lot of space and may be bigger than the actual message. A good guideline is to restrict a signature to your name, title and institution. Beware of including personal information, particularly telephone numbers or addresses since this information will be open to all recipients.

Adding your 'signature' to a message

Keeping an address book

As your collection of e-mail correspondents increases, a method of organisation becomes useful. Most e-mail programs have some form of address book function; Eudora calls these Nicknames. A nickname can represent one or many addresses. For example, all your contacts in one LEA could be grouped under the nickname 'Derbyshire'. Addressing a message 'To: Derbyshire', will result in it being sent to all your addressees in that group. However, there is a caveat. The e-mail addresses of all the members of a nickname will appear with the message when it is delivered. So, if a nickname has 50 members, all 50 e-mail addresses will appear before the message header, which can be a bit off-putting. However, there is a solution: 'copying to' other addressees instead.

Your software should have a 'CC' feature, which means sending a 'Carbon Copy' to other people. Addressees added to this line will receive your message as well as those on the 'To' line. They will see the addresses of all the others it has been copied to. There may be times, however, when you wish to conceal the fact that you are copying your messages to others and you can select 'BCC', which means 'Blind Carbon Copy'. Addressees added here will receive a copy of the message but the header will not contain

Picking up mail

Try to log on to your ISP every day – unlike post which is visible, you won't know if you've been sent urgent e-mails until you log on

Section 2 - Getting started with e-mail

the addresses of all the others it has been sent to. Hence, this is particularly useful when sending a message to many people or a nickname. So, for example, if you entered 'BCC: Derbyshire' everyone under the nickname Derbyshire would receive the message but they would not see a list of all the other recipients.

Anticipating difficulties

There are a finite number of connections to your service provider. At particular times of the day they will be busy; be patient and try again later. Between your machine and those you mail, there is a great deal of technology: telephone lines, modems and computers. From time to time some of it will fail and breakdowns are often unannounced and unavoidable. If you continue to experience problems, contact your service provider's help line, although it is quite likely that their telephone will be busy. A fax to them is a good idea, as it allows you to describe the problem in detail, which will be appreciated by the technical support team. If a service interruption is anticipated, you may receive a message as you connect to your service provider or they may put a notice on their Home page or their Usenet Newsgroup.

Junk mail

One of the penalties of electronic communication is that you are likely to receive 'junk mail'. This is particularly

likely if you subscribe to a mailing list. 'Spamming' is the term used to describe the practice of sending such mail and generally involves individuals or organisations mailing messages to hundreds of mailing lists, regardless of the interests of those lists. Some junk mail may be offers of pornographic material, but it's usually easy to spot this from the title and deal with it accordingly.

Joining mailing lists

Mailing lists enable a group of people to exchange e-mail about a subject that interests them and there are thousands of them, discussing virtually every subject and topic under the sun. Many are of interest only to a few people or fanatics but, for example, there is a mailing list called ukschools where people with an interest in using the Internet in primary and secondary schools write to each other about relevant topics and useful Web sites or ask for help and advice. The majority of mailing lists are open to anyone to join but some are available only to members; although free, you have to 'subscribe' to a list and ask to join. Generally, to do this you have to send an e-mail to the mailing list mail server, as in the following example, based upon the special needs and information technology mailing list. Conversely, to leave a mailing list, you have to 'unsubscribe':

To: majordomo@ngfl.gov.uk
Subject: [leave blank]
[Message]:
subscribe senit   [or]   unsubscribe senit

All messages sent to a mailing list of which you are a member will appear in your mailbox automatically, and you will have to decide what to do with them: reply to them (and send that reply either to the entire list or just to the individual who sent them), save or delete them, or forward the information to someone else who is not on the mailing list.

Mailing lists can be moderated, unmoderated or partially moderated. Moderated lists are those which have a person (or team of people) in charge, who takes responsibility for ensuring that messages sent to the list are focusing on the topic and do not exceed agreed levels of decency. Conversely, unmoderated lists permit anyone to send a message without vetting it and hence offensive messages may arrive in your mailbox.

The majority of mailing lists are unmoderated and there are mailing lists which you would not wish your pupils to access. In an attempt to prevent children, particularly, from viewing inappropriate material, several ISPs (RM and CampusWorld, for example), offer filtered services whereby known offensive lists are blocked and access is denied.

Joining Usenet groups

Usenet is a collection of bulletin boards or newsgroups on the Internet. Newsgroups are discussion groups: a user sends a message to the newsgroup and it is stored centrally on a 'news server' and kept there for days, weeks, or months, depending upon how the news server is set up. The messages do not appear in your mailbox automatically (unlike messages from mailing lists) but you will have to ask to read them, and you cannot edit or delete them. Anyone can view newsgroups, provided they have suitable 'news reader' software. There are newsgroups covering any and every topic and interest. Examples of newsgroups of value to schools include the following:

- uk.education
- uk.education.schools-it
- school.teachers
- tw.k-12.primary.math

As a general rule, newsgroups prefixed 'alt' should be avoided if they may be viewed by pupils since these 'ALTernative' newsgroups tend to concern salacious or offensive topics. The ISPs offering filtered services are generally fairly ruthless in blocking newsgroups.

Summary and tips

- Always create, read, reply and edit e-mail messages off-line
- Always complete the 'Subject' line on e-mails you create
- When replying to a message, edit out any irrelevant information
- Try to keep messages short, succinct and to the point
- Always remember to disconnect from your service provider
- Log on to your mailbox regularly, at least twice per week
- Go through your mailbox regularly and spend time deleting/printing/saving messages
- Add the telephone number of your service provider to your BT 'Friends and Family' numbers to cut the cost of being on line
- If something does not work the first time, repeat the process and you may find it will the second time!
- Do not assume that each time the system does not respond/work it is your fault!

SENCO support

Becta manages an e-mail forum for special needs co-ordinators (send an e-mail to Darren_Maynes@becta.org.uk), where you can exchange information with other SENCOs

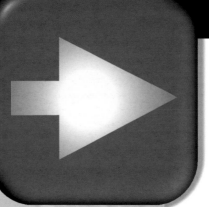

Everywhere you look these days you will see addresses of Web sites. They are at the end of films and TV programmes, in newspapers, on hoardings and even on lorries. Make a note of some you might like to look at or which may be useful.

Listed below are some Web addresses to start with:

- National Grid for Learning (http://vtc.ngfl.gov.uk)
- BBC (http://www.bbc.co.uk)
- Open Government (http://www.open.gov.uk)
- National Geographic magazine (http://www.nationalgeographic.com)
- NASA (http://www.nasa.gov).

If you want to access information on every subject under the sun, you will want to get onto the World Wide Web. Also known as WWW or simply the Web, this contains not only text-based information but sound, music samples, moving video and multimedia presentations too. Today, almost all organisations – including schools – are creating material for their own Web sites so that they can broadcast information about their services. This means that you can find educational material and information about art galleries

Section 3
Getting started with the World Wide Web

and museums, sport, travel, the latest films – virtually any topic you can think of.

Documents on the Web are called Web pages and anyone can create their own pages and launch them on the Web by holding them on a computer known as a server which is permanently connected to the Internet. There are already millions of sites on the Web, and so that some order exists, documents are keyworded so that you can search for the ones you want. 'Hot links' also exist between Web sites so that if you are on one site, you can click on a link and go automatically to other related sites.

Browsers

To view Web pages, you need a browser. This is a piece of software which fetches and composes material from the Web so that it can be read by your computer. The most common examples are Netscape and Internet Explorer. If you bought your computer recently, it may include a browser, or you may be able to download one from your Internet service provider.

To start your browser, connect up to the Internet and click the WWW button or menu item. Your browser window should open. The Netscape Navigator browser window is shown opposite, and most browsers will have similar features. It's important to update your browser from time to time, so that you can view all the features included in a Web page. Designers are increasingly using video and animation on the Web, and you may also need 'plug-ins' which will enable your browser to see the full effect; thesecan often be downloaded from the Web free of charge.

The Web contains more information than anyone could read in a lifetime, so the real problem is knowing where to look. There are several ways to find information but the most usual methods, particularly for those new to the system, are by using a 'search engine', entering the Web address of a site you know about and exploring from there, or using your ISP's home page to explore links.

Web spin-off

The World Wide Web was developed at CERN, the European laboratory for high-energy particle physics research in Switzerland

Search engines

Search engines collect and index vast numbers of pages from around the Web by keywording their contents. Some of the best known are Yahoo!, Excite, NLightN, Lycos and Alta Vista and you can use these search engines to find resources on virtually any subject. Most search engines work in a similar way, by asking you to enter a word or series of words which are then processed and a list of related links is returned to you as a Web page.

Frequently, the list may contain thousands of references and so, increasingly, search engines rank the links in order of relevance.

Example of a search engine screen showing a simple search

Search engines appear to be a burgeoning and developing part of the Web, so you may find it helpful to use just one or two of them in the early days of Web exploration to get a feel for how they operate and what sort of coverage they offer, since no one engine is able to offer access to the entire Web.

Entering a URL

You can also go to a specific page on the Web if you know the address or URL – Uniform Resource Locator – of that page. They all follow more or less the same format, so that in Becta's Web address (http://www.becta.org.uk), 'http://' denotes that it is a Web page , 'www.' denotes that it is on the World Wide Web, and 'becta.org.uk' shows that the page has been put together by the British Educational and Communications Technology Agency, an organisation in the UK.

To find addresses, look in Internet magazines, at the end of television programmes or in adverts, or ask friends and colleagues, but remember to copy them very carefully. As with e-mail addresses, the Web is not forgiving and one dot or letter out of place will mean failure. Sometimes you do not retrieve a page even with the correct address, and it may be that the URL has changed (which they do quite frequently and without warning). When this happens, you may be

routed to the new address automatically or merely told that the page could not be found, in which case you may have to try another tack – searching for the name using a search engine, for example.

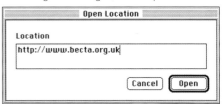

To find a page using a URL you may need to open a little window which is sometimes called the Location or Open Box. This is generally found by clicking on the 'File' menu. Type in the complete address, press return or click on 'OK' and the page should open for you.

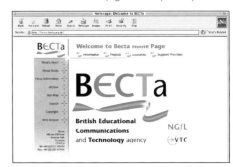

When you launch your browser, a Web page may automatically appear in its window. This may be your browser's or your service provider's 'home page'. This page, rather like the contents page of a book, allows you to see what is available on the other pages that make up a particular Web site. Any button or coloured or underlined text on a Web page denotes that these are links to other pages (or other sites) which you can look at. You will usually enter a Web site on its home page and may need to return to it not only to follow other links, but to leave the site.

Bookmarks

As you start to use the Web, you will find certain pages or sites which are really important to you and which you would like to access again. Rather than type in the URL each time, you can save the address.

To do this:
- Locate the desired page
- Click on 'Bookmarks' or 'Favorites' (usually found as a menu item on the top of the screen)
- Click on 'Add to Bookmarks' or 'Add to Favorites'.

When you want to find the page again:
- Connect to the WWW
- Click on 'Bookmarks/Favorites' (a list of saved pages will appear)

- Click on the desired page (the page will be called up automatically).

Logging off

When you have finished 'surfing the Net' you must log off. To do this, click on 'File' (at the top of the screen) and then choose 'Quit' from the menu. This will close your browser but you will still be connected to your service provider, so do not forget to disconnect when you have finished completely.

Progress checklist

	Yes	No
• Can you log on to the Internet?	☐	☐
• Can you type a URL?	☐	☐
• Can you launch a browser?	☐	☐
• Do you know how to use a search engine?	☐	☐
• Can you save an address as a bookmark/favourite site?	☐	☐
• Can you log off and disconnect?	☐	☐

World wide wait

You may find that Web connections are slower in the afternoons, because this is the time that users in the USA also log on; if possible, try to schedule your sessions for the mornings

Section 3 - Getting started with the World Wide Web

Finding information on the Web

The World Wide Web offers users a vast quantity of information, in a whole range of formats. Unfortunately, its chief advantage can also be its chief drawback, unless you know how to search effectively. To make the most of the services available via the Internet – and best use of your time – you need to use a range of search tools and techniques.

Using search engines

Each search engine now offers a level of help in the form of 'advanced searching techniques' or 'power searching' which enables you to define your searches more precisely. Different search engines use similar, but not necessarily the same, conventions but they all allow you to combine words in some way in a bid to narrow down or extend your search. However, since the vast majority of the information available via the Web is not formally indexed and grouped (as is the case for commercial databases) these extra facilities cannot overcome fully the difficulties this creates.

For example, using the search engine HotBot to find sites on the 'Tudors' will offer about 1,100 sites, ranked in order of relevance to the word. However, as you can see from the picture, of the first few sites, none of them is really relevant.

Consequently, you need to think more precisely about your information needs; what exactly is it that you want to know – about specific people? Society in general? Brick buildings? Hampton Court, in particular? Furthermore, you need to consider the likely outcome of searching the Web using broad search terms. For example, although changing fairly fast, the information available via the Internet is still very heavily biased towards America – so is it likely that Tudors will be viewed in the same way as in the UK? Conversely, what do you think might happen if you search using only the word 'volcanoes'? (Try it and see!)

The efficiency of your search techniques will thus have a direct bearing on the success of your searches on the Internet. The enormous quantity of poorly indexed information available via the Internet makes this an imperative, or you may spend a large sum of money on telephone calls for very little return. It not only pays to plan a search beforehand (that is, before you connect to your server), but it often makes sense to plan your search on paper, jotting down key words or phrases which will help to identify useful sites. And if developing effective search techniques is important for you, it is even more important for pupils, so that maximum results can be obtained with the minimum time and cost.

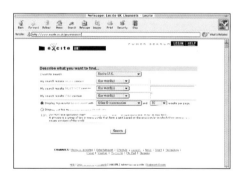

It may be best to restrict yourself initially to using only one or two search engines, so that you – and your pupils – can become adept at using the power searching techniques of those services. Once you have mastered the skills and concepts of searching, it's fairly easy to transfer the techniques to other search engines, even if they use different conventions, such as using '+' or 'AND' for those words which must appear in the search results. Sometimes, even when you have mastered search techniques, there will be occasions when there is just so much information available on a topic that no amount of refining the search will result in a reasonably small number of links.

In this case, you may choose to view only the first few sites listed and forget about the rest. This is particularly true if pupils are searching for information, since they are likely to be very restricted in the time they are able to spend on line. The table below gives some idea of the quantity of information available, and the coverage of some of the search engines.

Search Engine	Radio Waves	Tudors	Volcanoes
AltaVista	100,000	1,686	10,785
Excite	1,009,742	715	22,250
HotBot	83,035	1,100	1,644
InfoSeek	1,442,548	1,123	56,156
Lycos	5,300	118	6,033
Yahoo!	60	74	93

Menu searching

A menu-based search is another way of finding specific information. This divides the information on the Web into topic areas. Starting with a series of topic menus for you to choose from, it gradually narrows down the topic area. Once you have worked your way through the menus, click on the hypertext (underlined) link of the item that interests you.

What's new?

The Web is expanding so rapidly that hundreds of new sites come on line every day. To help keep users up to date, there are now Web pages entirely devoted to listing what is new. Some of these are a collection of all the new pages, whilst others list the URLs (addresses) of pages that the service thinks are worth visiting.

Your browser or ISP's main menu may have a button or menu item that displays a regularly updated list of new sites. This will contain hypertext links that will take you straight to the Web pages they have found. In Netscape Navigator, for example, there's a 'What's Cool' button and a 'What's New' button.

On-line discussion groups and newsgroups are a good source of up-to-date information on new sites for particular interests. Alternatively, there are newsgroups (comp.Internet.net happenings is one example) that are specially set up to discuss new sites.

Search techniques

You can narrow down or widen your Web search by using 'Boolean operators' – words like AND, OR and NOT (sometimes + or – in place of AND or NOT). Using AND will narrow down the search because it only finds entries which contain both keywords. Using OR will widen it, and NOT will narrow it further by excluding a keyword. You can also use 'wild cards' – often an asterisk (*) – so that if you enter 'educ*' it will find education, educational and educated.

desktop publishing. These include issues such as access and health and safety, but there are some additional issues too, so we take a brief look at them below.

Health and safety

The computer should be just one of many tools available to teaching and learning, and using it should be a comfortable and enjoyable experience. Take care when siting computers so that there are no trailing leads which pupils (and teachers) can trip over. Other good places to avoid are the sink and wet play area, for obvious reasons, and any area which means that there will be glare on the screen which will make viewing difficult.

If you have the choice of location, try to find a place in the classroom where you can easily see the screen while pupils are working alone on computer, but where their activity will not be too much of a distraction for the others.

Section 4

Some issues to consider

Seating is important, too. Ideally, the top of the monitor should be roughly in line with the user's eye-level, and the mouse at the same height as the user's elbow, so you may have to investigate higher bench seating which will enable this. Take care also that if you are using sound or talking screen-reading software, that it can be heard by pupils with known hearing difficulties; use of headphones may help to overcome this (particularly if they have individual volume controls) but you need to be aware of hygiene here and also that the use of headphones can be an isolating experience.

To help younger pupils and those with visual impairments, you should check the readability of Web pages and set your browser to your own preferences. Black text on a yellow background is probably the clearest, with text set at 14 or 18 points.

Access for all

There are a number of things you can do to enhance your time on-line and enable access for all learners:

- Get the fastest modem you can afford: this will speed up the time it takes to access the Web and reduce frustration
- Unless you specifically want to see the images on a Web page, use the option in your browser to turn them off: this will make downloading much faster
- If you can afford one, obtain a large-screen monitor so that a larger group of pupils can be involved in Internet searching and sending e-mail at one time
- Use an alternative input device rather than a mouse, such as a trackerball: this may be easier for young pupils and those with problems with motor control.

Controlling access to undesirable material

There has recently been a great deal of discussion in the media about computer pornography being accessible to children and young people, particularly via the Internet. There is also material which is undesirable for other reasons: it may be racist, provoke violence towards certain sectors of society or contain political views which most of us would consider highly unpleasant. However, deciding to avoid using the Internet for fear of coming across undesirable material is as unreasonable as deciding not to read books because a few feature pornographic sex or gratuitous violence. Even with unfiltered access to the Internet, you are unlikely to stray accidentally into undesirable areas, and for pupils who might be attracted by the very fact that undesirable material is there, there are strategies for dealing with their curiosity.

Screening sites

If you want greater control of the areas of the Web that your pupils can access, you can install screening software such as Net Nanny or Cyber Patrol, and set it up to your own requirements

Section 4 - Some issues to consider

The advice that follows is currently more appropriate to secondary schools but, as the use of the Internet increases, it will also be applicable to primary schools. Although you may not be planning to allow your pupils to access the Internet on their own just yet, in the near future pupils will expect to consult the Internet in the same way as they use reference books today. First, however, there are some specific issues relating to computer access of undesirable material, whether it is pornography, racist views or an incitement to violence, and whether it is accessed from the Internet or from disk:

- The content of material held on a computer disk is not immediately apparent
- Once obtained, material can be easily copied for further distribution
- Screen displays and material held on disk can be hidden with a key stroke, thus concealing the evidence
- Computer images can be easily altered and animated so that offensive or violent images can be produced to order
- With a modem it is possible to access and transfer material from almost anywhere in the world.

Teachers also need to be aware of a particular danger relating to pupils accessing material which is produced by extreme groups such as the National Front: Web sites and other printed matter can often appear to be 'official' and therefore lend a credibility to content which is untrue or at the very least, seriously biased. Two strategies may help here: first, an awareness of the type of material which pupils are gaining access to and second, teaching pupils how to appraise critically all the material they come across by assessing its accuracy and bias.

What can schools do?

There are a number of strategies available to schools for ensuring that pupils do not make a practice of obtaining or distributing undesirable material. Many Internet service providers can offer filtered access to the Internet, and other software utilities exist which may be added to a school network, but both of these may in fact limit pupils from carrying out legitimate searches of the Internet. Supervision of pupils is also a key factor, particularly where pupils have free access to computers out of lesson time, but few teachers will have the time or the inclination to peer over their pupils' shoulders at all times to ensure that their use of the Internet is appropriate.

Many schools find that a two-pronged attack is more effective, because it teaches pupils to exercise a sense of responsibility. The first is to hold open discussions with pupils about what constitutes offensive or undesirable material and why it is unacceptable; the second is to draw up a pupil contract for using computers in general and the Internet in particular, which looks at wider issues including security, copyright, backing up files and sociable network use.

Awareness is the key factor here: schools need to be alert to any signs of pupils behaving in an unacceptable way, and work to raise pupils' awareness of potential dangers. Schools will need to:

- develop pupils' understanding of implications of IT for working life and society
- alert parents to any problems relating to computer pornography or other undesirable material
- make sure that teachers can explain the arguments against pornography to pupils
- help parents to understand more about IT themselves – perhaps by running courses for them, or discussing with them the IT capability requirements of the National Curriculum
- make sure that parents and teachers know how and where to report incidents
- be seen to be regularly checking files held on networks
- supervise carefully the sharing of computer disks between home and school
- make sure that telecommunications links are closely managed

- be aware that where a child's behaviour at school indicates serious problems at home, they may be a need to involve social service departments
- bear in mind that precocious or otherwise inappropriate sexual behaviour may be a sign that a child is being abused (advice on the procedures to be followed by schools where this is so is contained in DFE Circular 4/88 'Working Together under the Children Act').

If you find material on the Web which you think is illegal or offensive, report it to The Internet Watch Foundation (tel: 01223 236077 or http://www.internetwatch.org.uk).

Home computers and children: some advice for parents

IT is now integral to children's learning and has a significant role in the National Curriculum. Many parents are aware of this and, to support their children's education, are buying computers for their children to use at home. This has many advantages but it can also cause problems which parents and schools need to deal with. Many schools are approached by parents seeking advice not only on buying computers, but also on how to 'manage' them; this section looks at some of the areas which may need to be addressed.

The power of new technology means that undesirable images and text can be introduced easily and unobtrusively to computers, through telephone links or simply by way of floppy disks. Computers can also be used to run games. While there are positive aspects to computer games, such as their potential to help children to think and act more quickly and to concentrate for longer, they can contain violent material, and children can play them in obsessive ways. Fortunately, there are a number of strategies for dealing with the problems, chief amongst which is being aware (as a parent or a teacher) of what is that children are using the computer for. Parents need to know that children could obtain undesirable computer-generated material by:
- sending for it by mail order
- buying it in the street or swapping it in the playground
- getting it from the Internet.

Strategies for ensuring this doesn't happen include:
- bringing the computer into the living room
- taking an interest in what children are doing with the computer
- asking children to show them how it works and explaining how they use computers in school
- making sure that computing and playing video games playing are only two activities among many that their children enjoy.

Censoring the Web

If you're using screening software, beware of censoring all sites with the word 'sex' in them: you'll also exclude all information on Essex, Middlesex and sextuplets as well

Section 4 - Some issues to consider

Parents also need to be aware that computers linked to telephones can run up large bills, and that if their children have access to a credit card, they could use it to buy material (appropriate or not) without them knowing.

It's also a good idea for parents to be ready to talk about pornography or violence with their children if these issues come up. Children are likely to be attracted to anything which they think is 'forbidden fruit', so a more effective strategy may be to discuss with them what pornography is and why people object to it; this way, children are more likely to form balanced opinions and set standards which they will apply to any new material they meet.

Further advice

Becta has produced an advice leaflet for parents, *Home Computers and Children – advice for parents on sensitive issues,* and multiple copies of this are available free of charge to schools on request.

The advice leaflet is also included in Becta's *Information Pack for Parents,* which offers much wider advice to parents who may be considering buying a computer for the home. The information sheets in this pack are freely photocopiable for use by schools and the pack costs £3.50. A video, lasting 10

minutes, showing computer activities which parents and children can undertake together and which reinforces the advice given in the pack is also available at a cost of £7.50. For further information telephone the Sales Department at Becta on (01203) 416994.

PIN (Parents Information Network) produces a very helpful free guide, *The Internet: an introduction for families.* PIN, PO Box16394, London, SE1 3ZP or e-mail post@pin-parents.com

The British Computer Society also has advice for schools on this subject. British Computer Society, tel: (+44) 01793 417417 fax: (+44) 01793 480270. http://www.bcs.org.uk

NCH Action for Children also produces a useful guide aimed at children using the Internet at home. Contact NCH Action For Children, 85 Highbury Park, London N5 1UD, tel: 0171 226 2033 fax: 0171 226 2537 http://www.nchafc.org.uk/

Norfolk County Council has published a series of booklets for IT Co-ordinators in schools covering a number of issues. The series is called Organising IT in Schools and includes a booklet about computer pornography. Contact Norfolk Educational Press, tel: (01603) 433276 fax: (01603) 700236.

Other local education authorities may also have prepared advice for schools about computer issues involving parents. Contact your IT Adviser for more information.

Copyright

The ability to copy material from electronic sources – the Web and CD-ROM, for example – raises a number of issues about copyright. This is a complex area, and for guidance, see the information on Becta's Web site (http://www.becta.org.uk).

Viruses

Viruses, which are programs deliberately designed to cause havoc in computer systems, have been around for some years. They are most commonly passed on by floppy disks but can also be spread via the Internet as users download software. Whilst it is still very rare for users to acquire a virus in this way, they can be difficult to detect. You need to be aware of this problem and take precautions to reduce the possibilities of downloading such unwelcome visitors. Accessing reputable sites only will help, for example, but it is wise to take other precautions.

Virus-checking software is readily available and should be used regularly; this is particularly necessary where pupils are allowed to bring disks in from home. Any files on the computer should be backed up regularly – a necessary precaution in case of computer or network failure in any case. If access to the Internet is via the school network, then schools really do need to consider proper protection, perhaps by installing a 'firewall' which offers a high degree of protection against viruses and outsiders hacking into the computer system.

Netiquette

There are standards of behaviour and conventions in using e-mail as there are in any other conversation. Keep your messages short, otherwise people will get bored and will delete your messages without reading them. If you are replying to/adding to a prolonged discussion, it sometimes helps to set the context for your comments so that people can catch up on previous correspondence. When you join any on-line group there is always a Frequently Asked Questions (FAQ) file about the group and the rules which apply.

You can use the on-line systems to broadcast a file or message to many people, such as details of a conference, but take care that you send it to appropriate individuals, mailing lists or newsgroups or there is a danger that recipients may view it as junk mail and send it straight back to you and fill up your mailbox with hundreds of copies of your own message.

When speaking, we moderate our messages by our tone, to show whether we are joking or serious, and there are ways of indicating this on e-mail. For example, you can create what are known as smileys, which use normal keyboard characters to create a picture of a face as you are writing. These are the most common ones:

:-)	Happy
:-D	Laughing
:-(	Sad
:-||	Angry
:-o	Shocked
;-)	Winking

Of course, sometimes you may just want to shout, and you can do this on e-mail by typing in CAPITAL LETTERS, but as with spoken conversation, this should be used sparingly.

Copying from the Web

All Web pages should have a copyright statement on them, saying whether you can incorporate material into your own work; if you cannot, then you will be infringing their copyright

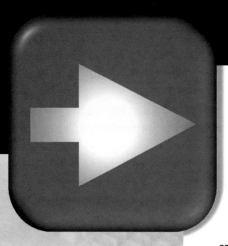

The Internet is not just a resource for teaching, it is a resource for teachers too. The Government has stated that all its communication with schools after the year 2002 will be in electronic form. No more reams of paper to plough though, no more forest devastation. It sounds like a good idea, but if it is to work, teachers need to develop a new mind set, a new approach to the search for resources for teaching and curriculum development. Increasingly we will come to see the Internet at the first place to go for ideas on how to teach concepts, for extra worksheets to reinforce some of the basics, for extension work for able pupils or for ways of developing the school's schemes of work.

This is what the National Grid for Learning is all about. The intention is that the Grid will be a way of finding and using on-line learning and teaching materials. To find all of these resources, teachers will need to be able to search the Internet or find a 'trusty friend' in the form of a Web site which can offer support in the form of a substantial resource bank or a gateway to other appropriate sites.

Section 5

The Projects

The three projects which follow illustrate a variety of ways in which the Internet may be used in primary education. They make use of both key Internet facilities – e-mail and the World Wide Web – in the context of three areas of the curriculum: mathematics, English and science.

All three projects aim to illustrate and make use of the strengths of the Internet. Each project contains ideas which can be used throughout the school, addressing the needs of children from Reception to Year 6 and the needs of teachers from Internet novices to those with substantial confidence and experience. The science and English projects focus on using the Internet with children, while the mathematics project looks at its potential as a resource for teachers.

Project 1 –
Developing Mathematics

This project is about using the Internet in three different ways to support mathematics teaching and learning. The first activity is about downloading classroom materials such as worksheets in the form of files which may be printed out directly or edited to customise them for your own circumstances. The second activity is about finding materials to help develop the whole-school mathematics curriculum, in this case by getting

parents involved. The third activity is about differentiation – in particular, finding resources for the enrichment of children who are particularly able.

The three sites referred to in this project differ substantially in their sophistication and presentation but each provides a useful resource in its own way. The third site, furthermore, is a suitable candidate for the 'trusty friend' which can be visited again and again and which can lead you to a treasure trove of mathematics on the Net.

The three activities in this project are not in any way sequential, but present three different approaches to the use of materials accessed through the Internet. Each offers resources appropriate to children of all ages.

Maths Activity 1 – Downloading Activity Sheets
Commercial mathematics schemes and text books cannot possibly cater for all the needs of all children. Able pupils may complete a page of work quickly and have time left over for enrichment and extension activities, while the less able may need more practiceof basis skills than the books provide. There are a number of different Web sites which provide materials for teachers in a form which can be downloaded to the computer's hard disk and later printed out as activity sheets.

Section 5 - The Projects

Mathsphere is an example of this type of site. It supplies mathematical worksheets for basic skills practice for children at Key Stages 1 and 2. These range from number line problems to develop understanding of and fluency with subtraction in Year 1, to work on square and cube numbers for pupils at the top end of the primary school. The site also provides a magazine of mathematical activities for primary pupils and a monthly competition with a seasonal flavour.

You can access Mathsphere at
http://www.mathsphere.co.uk/home.html

The activity sheets are chosen from an on-screen menu but instead of appearing on the screen of your Internet browser, they are sent to your hard disk in the form of PDF (Portable Document Format) files. This ensures that the page layout and design is retained exactly as the author intended so as to provide activity sheets with an attractive layout which can be printed and used directly. Each short file takes just a few minutes to arrive and your browser will handle the process automatically, perhaps asking you to specify where you wish the file to be stored or else placing it directly on the desktop. Many browsers show a download window as the file arrives which indicates how long the process will take.

In order to view and print these materials it is necessary to have a program called Adobe Acrobat Reader, which is also freely available and can be downloaded in the same way. This takes a little longer (20–30 minutes) so it is best to set it going before taking a coffee break. Downloading files in this way is a straightforward matter and support for novice users is provided on the site.

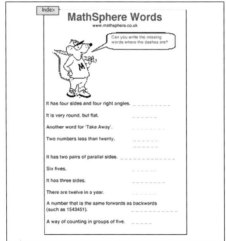

A typical worksheet from Mathsphere

Once you have the files and the software to read them, they can be opened in the usual way and will

appear as fully designed worksheets on your screen which can be printed directly from the program. It is not possible to edit the worksheets directly, but both text and graphics can be copied and pasted into any other suitable application and then freely manipulated (use the Tools menu to select whether you wish to copy text or graphics).

Maths Activity 2 – Getting Parents Involved

Many schools have begun to draw on parental support for the mathematical development of their children. With the government advocating an increased amount of homework for primary pupils, many home–school links are being established. There is an American Web site called Helping Your Child Learn Math which offers not only a source of good ideas but also a short booklet to explain to parents why and how they can help with children's mathematical development, and activities which children and parents can do together at home.

You can access Helping Your Child Learn Math at
http://www.ed.gov.pubs/parents/Math/index.html

This is a very old site (in Internet terms) which was set up in 1994 and this is apparent from the lack of graphics or design. The material is basically a book transferred to the screen and is perhaps best read from printed copy. Your Internet browser will enable you to print it out.

The book starts with a rationale aimed at non-mathematical parents which explains what mathematics is, expanding the definition from basic arithmetic (which is what many parents recognise as mathematics), to incorporate problem solving, communicating mathematically and reasoning. Although the language is American, the content is very sound and fully in line with the National Curriculum approach to mathematics, particularly Using and Applying. The ages described are also in terms of American grades (kindergarten to 8th grade) but the grades map well against the year groupings of the National Curriculum, with kindergarten equivalent to Reception and grades 1 to 6 equivalent to primary Year 1 to Year 6.

Rather than simply using the Web site's booklet, you may prefer to prepare your own pamphlet by cutting and pasting from the American materials into your own word processor or desktop publishing package. It is obviously far cheaper to carry out this work off-line, so you should save the Web pages to a file on your hard disk. There are two ways to do this:

• Click on Save As from the File menu in your browser and you will then be prompted to choose a name and location to save the current page
• Alternatively, choose Download File from the same menu, in which case you will be asked to type in the URL of the file you wish to download and again specify where you wish it to be saved.

The first of these is perhaps the simpler method, as there is no need to type in the URL. In either case, the file can then be opened from your browser while off-line and sections cut and pasted into any suitable application. Each Web page must be saved separately.

The site also contains a set of activities for parents and children to carry out at home, and you could incorporate these into your pamphlet or produce separate homework sheets, perhaps enhanced with your own clip art.

An alternative strategy for copying individual pieces of text from Web sites into your documents is to use the computer's clipboard (while on-line) in just the same way as you would when cutting and pasting between any two application programs off line. Select the text in the on-line document and choose Copy from the edit menu. This places the text onto the clipboard. Now open a word processor (or scrapbook) window and paste the text in place.

Section 5 - The Projects

Maths Activity 3 – Differentiation/Enrichment

Useful though both of the above sites are, neither is wide ranging enough to serve as the 'trusty friend' who will lead you on to exploring more places on the Internet where you may go to develop your mathematics teaching. For this you need the Primary Section of the Nrich site, set up by the University of Cambridge School of Education.

You can find it at
http://www.nrich.maths.org/primary/index.html

The Nrich Project aims to establish a permanent national centre for curriculum enrichment to provide mathematical learning support for very able children of all ages. The learning and enjoyment of mathematics is promoted through an Internet newsletter and the participation of university students as peer teachers, providing an electronic answering service. The centre offers support, advice and in-service training to teachers and resources for mathematics clubs.

Although the focus is on very able pupils, the Primary section of the site offers activities suitable for whole classes and a variety of mathematical and strategic games which are of value across the ability range.

These are changed regularly and have a seasonal flavour when appropriate (in December all activities were linked to Christmas, for example).

There are challenges for children at Key Stages 1 and 2, a Kids Magazine full of mathematics titbits and a richly resourced teachers' area with notes about all the activities and articles about various aspects of mathematics teaching.

A mathematical dictionary is provided and it is also possible to search the site by keyword or mathematical category. There are also e-mail facilities, which allow users to send in answers to any of the problems or challenges, or ask for help with any mathematical query.

The site also contains an extensive set of links to other mathematical Internet sites where articles, games and activities may be found. Nrich is thus a good starting point in the quest for materials or advice: if there is nothing on the Nrich site itself there is a gateway to other possible sources. The links are well annotated with a short explanation of what each site comprises and range from those which cover very specific activities (About Today's Date or The World of Escher) to general information sites such as that of the ATM (Association of Teachers of Mathematics).

There is also a little corner for mathematics Web pages which have been set up by schools both in the UK and overseas which might just inspire you to tackle something similar yourself (you will probably need to consult your software manual to do this).

Nrich is a superb site which you will want to visit again and again, so be sure to add it to your list of favourites bookmarks. The best way to develop your mathematics teaching used to be to attend a working weekend run by one of the mathematical associations. Now, although lonelier, you can achieve almost all the same objectives by sitting in front of your computer.

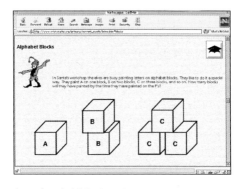

A page from the Nrich primary site

Project 2 -
Developing English

A variety of initiatives over the past two years have set out to create a national climate in which reading is highly valued. Literate pupils must not merely be able to read, they should be interested in books (fiction and non-fiction), read with enjoyment and be able to evaluate and justify their reading preferences.

The book review is an old stalwart of the primary curriculum. There can be few children who have never written at least one and few teachers who have not read far too many. The task of producing a book review is not bad as writing tasks go, as there is a clear audience and purpose: the audience is the teacher and the purpose is to help her keep abreast of what (or whether) all the children in the class are reading.

But in the real world, book reviews are for sharing – telling the readers enough about a book to allow them to decide whether or not they wish to read it for themselves. The framework for the National Literacy Strategy assumes that, from an early age, children will be evaluating what they read and expressing opinions about their likes and dislikes. These opinions should be shared – at first with classmates, later with children in other schools (in the UK and abroad).

In the middle years of the primary school, children can begin to take an interest in book reviews written by others – not just their peers but also adult reviewers of children's books who might be more skilled than children at encapsulating the theme or story. They will have a growing interest in authors and publishers and should by now have identified which authors they like to read and what types of books interest them.

Older children will be able to review their reading with greater sophistication and articulate their personal response to literature. They will be able to contribute constructively to shared discussion about literature, responding to, and building on, the views of others. They will also be able to evaluate non-fiction texts for their contents and usefulness (including texts on media such as CD-ROM or the Internet).

This project is about using ICT do all of those things. Some of the ideas are for off-line activities using overlay keyboards, word-processing templates and writing frames, for example. Other ideas use e-mail (to share book reviews with other schools or communicate directly with authors or publishers) and the World Wide Web for looking at sites which provide information about books (ranging from other schools' Web sites which may run a book of the month section, through to publishers' own sites which trail forthcoming publications). Ultimately books can be ordered on-line (by teachers or by pupils

Section 5 - The Projects

under supervision) enabling interesting new books to be swiftly acquired.

The activities described below have been planned for the early, middle and later years of the primary school. They represent a gradual increase in use of ICT, in addition to a development in English work. However, activities suggested for younger pupils could be adapted at Key Stage 2 for pupils (or teachers) who are less comfortable with the use of ICT, particularly the Internet. You could, for example, fax or e-mail book reviews (to share these with other schools) instead of posting them on the school's Web site or a bulletin board.

In the activities, boxed text refers to the National Literacy Strategy.

English Activity 1 - Book of the Month
(R, Year 1, and 2)

Year 1 – Term 2	Text Level Work 3

…choose and read familiar books with concentration and attention, discuss preferences and give reasons;
After reading each big book, during shared text work of the Literacy Hour, spend a few minutes evaluating the book using the review sheet on page 38 or a similar template set up as a keyboard overlay, or My Word or Claris Works template. Features of the book which gave it appeal should be highlighted in some way (ring, tick, colour etc). Keep the completed form with the book (on display or stuck inside the front cover). At the end of each month, revisit all the books (and their review sheets) and discuss which has been the best book of the month. You might like to display this for parents or other classes with its review sheet.

Year 1 – Term 3	Text Level Work 4

… read with sufficient concentration to complete a text, and to identify preferences and give reasons;
When children have become familiar with the review sheet and its use, ask them to complete their own (individually or in groups) for books read at home or at school. Include these in the 'book of the month' competition.

Establish contacts with other schools (local, nationwide, or overseas) and swap information about each book of the month by faxing a photocopy of the book cover and a copy of the review sheet. Try to get hold of the books recommended by other schools and allow your pupils to make their own evaluation and compare it with the recommendation

Year 2 – Term 3	Text Level Work 12

…write simple evaluations of books read and discussed giving reasons;

Extend the review sheet or prepare on-screen templates for book reviews to reflect the growing capabilities of the pupils. Separate templates should be prepared for reviewing fiction and non-fiction books, as shown on pages 38 and 39. As you gain in confidence with ICT, use e-mail instead of fax to swap book of the month recommendations with other schools.

English Activity 2 - Authors (Years 2, 3 and 4)

Year 2 – Term 3	Text Level Work 4 & 5

…compare books by the same author: settings, characters, themes; to evaluate and form preferences, giving reasons;
…read about authors from information on book covers, e.g. other books written, whether author is alive or dead, publisher; to become aware of authorship and publication;
Help to direct children's attention to authors and encourage them to read cover notes about authors and to look out for other books by the same author.

Year 3 – Term 3	Text Level Work 9

…be aware of authors and to discuss preferences and reasons for these;
Talk about favourite authors. Allow children to access the Web sites of authors or publishers to find out

more about their favourite authors and about other books they have written. Information about forthcoming books is often also available.

Three good gateway sites (sites which give access to many authors' and publishers' own sites) are:

- Just for Kids who Love Books (http://www.geocities.com/Athens/Olympus/1333/kids.htm)
- OKUK Books (http://www.okukbook.com/)
- Children's Literature Web Guide (http://www.acs.ucalgary.ca/~dkbrown/index.html)

Encourage children to find the URLs of Web sites of specific authors and add these to lists of bookmarks or favourites so that they can be readily found by other children. Authors' sites can be found through the above gateways or by using a search engine.

Some authors have lovely sites which include activities for children and even sections on teaching ideas for using their books in class. Try, for example, Jan Brett's site (http://www.janbrett.com/).

Year 4 – Term 1	Text Level Work 8

… find out more about popular authors, poets etc. and use this information to move on to more books by favourite writers;

You can also share references to good authors' or publishers' Web sites with other schools though e-mail.

Ask children to read and evaluate reviews of children's books written by adult reviewers. These are available on publishers' Web sites or in text-based materials such as the *Times Educational Supplement*. Does the review make the children want to read the book?

Most publishers have reviews of books on their sites, often with a picture of the front cover. Reviews usually include prices, which for American publishers are in dollars.

Year 3 – Term 3	Text Level Work 20

… write letters, notes and messages linked to work in other subjects, to communicate within school; letters to authors about books, selecting style and vocabulary appropriate to the intended reader;

You can also enable children to communicate directly with authors through their Web sites, as many have a facility to send messages. Get them to say what they think of the books or to ask questions, for example, about forthcoming publications or where the authors get their ideas for plots.

Section 5 - The Projects

English Activity 3 – Evaluating Texts

(Year 4, 5 and 6)

Year 4 – Term 3	Text Level Work 10

...describe and review own reading habits and to widen reading experience;

Year 5 – Term 3	Text Level Work 10

...write discursively about a novel or story, e.g. to describe, explain, or comment on it;

Year 6 – Term 1	Text Level Work 3

...articulate personal response to literature, identifying why and how a text affects the reader;

Year 6 – Term 1	Text Level Work 5

...contribute constructively to shared discussion about literature, responding to and building on the views of others;

Year 6 – Term 3	Text Level Work 11

...write a brief helpful review tailored for real audiences;

Use writing frames as shown on page 40 or free-form writing to expand the scope of children's reviews of literature. Encourage children to write about elements such as plot and characters, and about their own emotional response to the book. Get them to write for an audience of their peers. Share this work by posting it on your school's Web site or a publisher's Web site. Encourage children to read reviews written by other children and compare their responses.

Many publishers' Web sites invite readers to write reviews and post them on their notice board of Recent Customer Reviews. Some even provide guidelines for reviewers and reviews by other customers can be read. Try, for example http://www.amazon.com/

You could also set up a database of books. Discuss with pupils what information it should contain and the field structure. Share your data with other schools, via e-mail, to build up a larger database. Use it to find books with similar themes by different authors and to compare children's responses to these.

Year 3 – Term 2	Text Level Work 13

...discuss the merits and limitations of particular instructional texts, including IT and other media texts, and to compare these with others, where appropriate, to give an overall evaluation;

Year 4 – Term 2	Text Level Work 15

...appraise a non-fiction book for its contents and usefulness by scanning, e.g. headings, contents list;

Year 5 – Term 3	Text Level Work 14

...select and evaluate a range of texts, in print or other media, for persuasiveness, clarity, quality of information;

Year 6 – Term 1	Text Level Work 12

...comment critically on the language, style success of examples of non-fiction such as periodicals, reviews, reports leaflets;

Provide opportunities for children to evaluate non-fiction materials. Include information books and IT resources such as Web sites or CD-ROM. Ask them to discuss why some materials are better than others and to establish criteria for judging an effective information resource.

Share information about good information resources (good Web sites, for example) with other schools via e-mail or noticeboards, or by providing links on your own Web site. Involve children in looking at up-to-date information about best-sellers published on the Web. Lists are available of all-time best-sellers or best-sellers of the month or year. Use this to make purchasing decisions. The Children's Literature Web Guide (http://www.acs. ucalgary.ca/~dkbrown/index.html) for example, has several different best-seller lists (prices in dollars). Reviews are available for many of the books on the lists. You could also use the Web to order books directly on-line. Show children how this is done.

Review Sheet for Book of the Month

(suitable for R, Year I)

Title

Author

I like this book because

it is funny

it has rhyme

it has rhythm

it has good pictures

it has an interesting story

it is exciting

it taught me something new

it is about ...

Child's Name

Review Template for Fiction (suitable for Year 1,2,3)

Title

Author

Publisher

Fiction, Poetry or Non-Fiction

What is this book about?

Where does the story take place?

Who are the main characters?

Is it easy to read?

Why do you like (or not like) this book?

Other similar books that I have read

Child's Name

Review Template for Non-Fiction (suitable for Year 1,2,3)

Title _____

Author _____

Publisher _____

Fiction, Poetry or Non-Fiction

What is this book about?

Does it have a contents page?

Does it have an attractive cover?

Does it have an index?

Does it have clear pictures?

Does it have diagrams with labels?

Does it have clear headings?

Is it easy to find information?

Why do you like (or not like) this book?

Other similar books that I have read

Child's Name _____

Writing Frame for Literature Review (suitable for Years 4,5,6)

Title

Author   **Publisher**

Type of book   **Target Readers**

This book is about

The setting is

The main characters in the story are

The author writes in an interesting way. For example,

The book made me feel

The best part of the book was

I enjoyed reading (or did not enjoy) this book because

This book was similar to other books that I have read such as

The type of book that I most like reading is

I enjoy this genre because

Child's Name

Project 3 – Developing Science

Much of science is about identifying similarities and differences and seeking explanations as to why these occur. Thus, the very first unit of the DfEE recommended scheme of work for Science (Unit 1A, Ourselves) focuses on the similarities and differences between human beings. Later units, throughout the primary years, are concerned with moving out into the wider environment, establishing patterns of similarities and differences which define the three strands of science.

The Internet can support budding scientists in two ways: by providing a medium for sharing their findings and comparing data, and by giving access to scientific information which might not be readily available in books. Such information might include very recent developments in science, such as the discovery of water on the moon, or data which is ephemeral such as tide timetables. However, much of the scientific information available on the World Wide Web is not specifically written for children and may need to be interpreted by teachers before pupils are able to make much of it.

The first activity, for the youngest primary pupils, involves using ICT to share the information collected in the Ourselves study. The Internet provides an opportunity for sharing of data beyond the school boundaries, which can help children gain greater understanding about ways in which humans differ and are similar. This sharing can be by fax or by e-mail. If data is collected on the computer, files can be sent as attachments to e-mail messages and read by any school with the same software.

Sharing on a much larger scale becomes possible through managed Internet projects where someone takes on the responsibility for collating and organising the data. The activity for middle years involves looking at such a project and becoming involved at one of two levels: either simply as a user of the materials provided or as a full participant in the data collection programme.

The Earth, Sun and Moon unit from Year 5 is the context for the third activity, which compares day length in different parts of the world and highlights some Web sites of interest in this area.

The activities described below have been planned for the early, middle and later years of the primary school. They represent a gradual increase in use of ICT and are linked closely to the DfEE suggested scheme of work for science. Italicised text refers to this scheme of work.

Section 5 - The Projects

Activity 1 – Ourselves (R, Year 1, 2)

Unit 1A Ourselves
Ask children to suggest ways in which they differ. Help them to collect data about themselves, e.g. eye colour, size of feet, hair colour and to represent this using models e.g. a brick tower or charts.

Ask children to collect data about themselves such as eye colour, shoe size, hair colour, whether hair is straight or curly. For the youngest children, collect data which falls into discrete categories which remain the same throughout life (eye colour, for example) rather than a continuous range which must be measured and which will change as children grow, such as height. One more unusual difference which could be considered is the ability to roll the tongue.

It is important to use characteristics which will lead in later stages to understanding of inherited differences between children; for example, eye colour is suitable, where the colour of children's jumpers is not.

Record the data in the form of pictograms which may be generated on paper (by each child adding a sticker) or using a computer program. Discuss the findings.

You can then share this data, by fax, with schools in different parts of Britain or different parts of the world.

It will be necessary to grasp the nettle of racial differences when discussing why the population of some schools is more homogeneous than others. The development of racial understanding involves appreciating that although there are many variations in the appearance of different human beings, our similarities are far greater than our differences.

Unit 2C Variation
Ask children to compare the size of e.g. their hand with the hand of another child and discuss how they could be measured.

Year 2 children can begin to explore differences between individuals that are continuous and measurable such as hand span or height. They should understand that these characteristics also change throughout our lives, unlike those considered above. Again data can be graphed manually or using a computer graphing program.

You could swap data with other schools either by fax or by sending files as e-mail attachments (you'll need to check first that the recipient school has a copy of the software used to prepare the file).

Discuss the differences between schools in different parts of the world and begin to ask children to think about what makes a fair test. For example, it will only be valid to compare heights of children in the same age group.

Activity 2 – Environment (Years 2, 3 and 4)

Unit 4B Habitats
…make predictions of organisms that will be found in a habitat
…observe the conditions in a local habitat and make a record
…group organisms according to observable features
…use keys to identify local plants or animals

The Globe Programme is an international project which encourages schools all over the world to measure aspects of their local environment and share their findings through the Internet. It is aimed at the 8 to 14 age range, so it's suitable for children in the middle and upper years of the primary school.

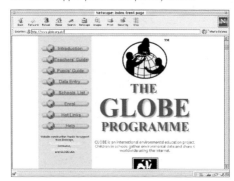

Home page of the Globe site

The project provides a complete teaching package with a full teachers' guide and sets of pupil worksheets which can be accessed on-line or printed. It is possible to use the materials at one of two levels. To begin with teachers may just wish to use the resources provided to structure a teaching programme linked to the Habitat Unit of the Science Scheme of Work. Later it is possible to enrol as a Globe teacher, attend a training session and send your data to become part of the massive international database which the project is building up.

You can access Globe at: http://www.globe.org.uk

The areas of study currently covered by the project are weather, water, soils and land cover. It is planned to introduce four further topics at a later stage in the project (transport, energy, waste and biodiversity).

It's best to start with just one area of study – Landcover fits best with the Habitat Unit of the Science scheme of work. Select the Pupil Guide section from the home page and look at the notes. These show how to set up a biology study site and how to investigate the ground vegetation and trees on the site. Plant identification keys are not provided but there are instructions for making simple instruments such as a densiometer tube for measuring canopy cover and a clinometer to measure tree height. The Teachers' Guide provides a rationale for the work.

It is not necessary to complete the survey with the rigour suggested in the activity sheets unless enrolled on the project. The materials contain many useful resources which can be tailored to requirements. (To cut and paste any part of the material, just highlight and use the Edit menu in the usual way; text may be pasted into any other suitable application.)

The full text of the Science Scheme of Work may be obtained via the Internet and downloaded as a PDF file. This means that the file is transferred to the hard disk of your computer over the telephone line and can later be read (or cut and pasted from) at leisure. The material is on the DfEE Standards Pages (http://www.standards. dfee.gov.uk) where there are also instructions for downloading files to your computer.

Other interesting Web sites related to habitat include that of the National Wildlife Federation (USA) which provides information about creating a natural wildlife habitat in school (http://www.nwf.org/nwf/habitats/ schoolyard), and the BugClub (http://www.ex.ac. uk/bugclub/) which includes an insect identification key.

Section 5 - The Projects

Activity 3 – Day Length (Years 4, 5 and 6)
Unit 5E Earth, Sun and Moon

…present times of sunrise and sunset in a graph and to recognise trends and patterns in the data.

Begin by asking children to make a note of the time it gets light in the morning and dark in the evening. Can they devise a fair test of this? If equipment to measure and log light intensity is available, a specific level can be chosen, otherwise a more rough and ready test will have to be devised (reading a specific sized print without artificial light, perhaps). Alternatively official times of sunrise and sunset can be found in diaries or newspapers or on the Internet (see below).

A resource sheet for teachers on 'Day and Night' is available through the Virtual Teacher Centre of the National Grid for Learning at http://vtc.ngfl.gov.uk/resource/cits/science/prfocus/psinvest/psiindex.html

Once the children have gathered data for several days, ask them to use it to calculate local daylength for a specific date. Pupils can also compare local data with data from other schools in different parts of the country and different parts of the world (on the same date). Data can be exchanged by e-mail and plotted on maps.

You could also set up a more systematic study of daylength around the world. Begin by looking at variations in daylength in different parts of the UK. From sunrise and sunset times in different cities and towns (obtained via the Web – see below) the total daylength can be calculated for each location. These can then be ranked in order (1 for the longest daylength, 2 for the next longest and so on). It will be found that the differences in daylength at different UK locations are not very great (approximately 1 hour's difference between the extremes).

The Web site http://www.worldtime.com is an excellent resource for this work. The first screen presents a globe and by clicking on the appropriate spot, the map shown can be recentred on the UK or any other world location. The map shows which parts of the world are in daylight and darkness at the time of viewing by the position of shadow on the map. When the map is centred on the UK, data is available for the times of sunrise and sunset in 15 different UK cities.

You will probably need to explain that because this country is relatively small, daylength does not differ dramatically from place to place. To spot patterns in the differences and similarities between daylengths in different places it is necessary to use a larger area of the globe. The US provides a good testbed, for which much data is available. You could collect information about daylength in US cities, for the current date, using the worksheet on page 47. After ordering the data, as above, get the children to plot it on a map of the US. Work through the cities in rank order (longest day to shortest day) writing the daylength beside each location on the map. Ask the children to try to identify a pattern as they work. It should be possible for children to deduce that locations on similar latitudes have similar daylengths whereas different latitudes have different daylengths. Depending on the time of year, daylength will either increase or decrease as locations progress north or south.

Data about daylength in US cities is available from a number of sites.One of the most useful is the US Naval Observatory site (http://aa.usno.navy.mil/AA/data/docs/RS_OneDay.html). The date shown can be set to the current date and FORM A used to obtain sunrise and sunset times for US locations. It is necessary to identify State as well as city name, which is why this has been given on the worksheet.

Other sites which supply similar information are Jarmo's Solar Calculator (www.netti.fi/~jjlammi//sun.html). This site has six US cities available through the menu (starred on the worksheet on page 47). The advantage of this site is that daylength is calculated automatically.

Another alternative is http://www.jabberwocky.com/photo/suntimes.html. This site has very detailed data with locations pinpointed to individual towns, accessed via Counties within States, which may make it difficult to use with a standard (UK) atlas. However, the site does contain information about the current time of day at that location which is of additional interest. Try New York in New York County of New York State or, similarly, Oklahoma City in Oklahoma County of Oklahoma State.

Once children have begun to develop the idea that daylength may be related to latitude, this may be further tested using the second part of the US Navy site. Here locations are specified by entering latitude and longitude positions. Children can begin by entering figures for known locations or could simply explore the relationship of daylength to latitude, holding longitude and time zone constant (that is, set to 0). This will allow them to verify their hypothesis that daylength is related to latitude. At latitude 0 (the Equator) daylength will be approximately 12 hours. As latitude increases to 80 (polar circles, north or south) daylength can be seen to increase to 24 hours or decrease to zero (depending on time of year). In this case, data for sunrise and sunset is not available. Children may need help in interpreting the note 'Missing Sun phenomena indicate Sun above (below) horizon for extended period of time', that is, the Sun never rises (or sets).

Using the US Naval Observatory site (http://aa.usno.navy.mil/AA/data/docs/RS_OneDay.html) FORM B can be used to obtain sunrise and sunset times for any location specified by latitude and longitude.

Discuss the Land of the Midnight Sun and Polar Winters where the sun never rises. Explore what happens to daylength in different locations at different times of the year by altering the date at the top of FORM B. It should readily be discovered that on the Equator, daylength is a constant 12 hours all year round. As distance from the pole increases, daylength becomes more variable throughout the year. Good dates to investigate are the equinoxes, June 21st (the longest day in the northern hemisphere and the shortest day in the southern hemisphere) and December 21st (the shortest day in the northern hemisphere and the longest in the southern).

A globe and a strong light will help to model the rotation of the Earth on a tilted axis to explain why these variations occur and discuss seasonal differences. Ask children to show other ways of modelling this too, by using themselves as Sun and Earth or by drawing or using other models. Secondary sources such as video or CD-ROM are also helpful in illustrating the Earth spinning on its axis.

Section 5 - The Projects

Daylight throughout the UK

City	Sunrise (time)	Sunset (time)	Day length (hrs)	Order (1 = longest)
Belfast				
Birmingham				
Bristol				
Cardiff				
Coventry				
Edinburgh				
Glasgow				
Leeds				
Liverpool				
London				
Manchester				
Middlesbrough				
Newcastle upon Tyne				
Nottingham				
Sheffield				

Child's Name

Daylight throughout the USA

State	City	Sunrise (time)	Sunset (time)	Day length (hrs)	Order (1 = longest)
California	Los Angeles				
Florida	Miami*				
Georgia	Atlanta				
Illinois	Chicago*				
Louisiana	New Orleans				
Michigan	Detroit*				
New York	New York*				
Oklahoma	Oklahoma City				
Tennessee	Memphis				
Texas	Houston*				
Utah	Salt Lake City				
Washington	Seattle*				

Child's Name _____

Section 6

Sources of further help

Becta has a wide range of information sheets on-line on its Web site (http://www.becta.org.uk) which cover the use of e-mail, the Internet and other ICT issues.

Journals

Internet Magazine Emap Business Communications
Tel: 0181 868 7616
http://www.emap.com/internet/home.htm

Internet Today Paragon Publishing
Tel: 01202 299900, http://www.paragon.co.uk/it/

Internet World VNU Business Publications
Tel: 0171 316 9000, http://www.iw.vnu.co.uk

. net Future Publishing, Tel: 01225 442244
http://www.futurenet.com/netweb/netmag/default.htm

Becta publications

Connecting schools, networking people: ICT planning, purchasing and good practice for the National Grid for Learning, Becta 1998

Education Departments' Superhighways Initiative (EDSI), information sheet, 1997 – free

Glossary of terms relating to IT, information sheet, 1997 – free

Internet searching, information sheet, 1997 – free

Parents and IT, information sheet, 1997 – free

Other publications

All you need to know about Internet jargon,
Davey Winder, Future Books, 1995

Children on the Internet: a parents' guide,
NCH Action for Children, 1996

Finding it on the Internet, Paul Gilster, Wiley, 1996

How to use the Internet, Heidi Steele, Ziff Davies, 1996

The Internet, John Levine, IDG Books, 1996

Internet and WWW: the rough guide,
Angus J. Kennedy, Penguin, 1996

Internet education: a guide, Cheryl Harris, Wadsworth, 1996

Internet for busy people, Christian Crumlish, Osborne, 1997

Internet for teachers, Brad Williams, IDG Books, 1996

Introducing the Internet, Lynne Evans, Pearson, 1996

New Internet business, Jill H. Ellsworth, Wiley, 1996

Schools online: Phase 1 – Final report, Department of Trade and Industry (DTI), 1997

Schools online project: summary of report of Phase 1, Department of Trade and Industry (DTI), 1997

Teaching and learning with the Internet,
Phil Moore (ed.), BT CampusWorld, 1995

UK guide to the Internet, Mike James, I/O Press, 1996

UK education Internet primer, Nicholas Mailer and Bruce Dickinson, Questions Publishing, 1997

Videos
A BBC guide to the Internet,
BBC Educational Developments, 1995

Internet: the Cyberian connection, Purple Training Ltd, 1995

Introduction to the Internet, Visual Edge Productions, 1995

Learners' guide to the Internet, SCET, 1997 (part of the SCET CyberSchools Initiative)

Teaching and Learning with IT, Becta

Software
Essential Internet starter kit (CD-ROM),
Koch Media Ltd, 1995

The Internet for absolute beginners,
Mike Lloyd, Aslib, 1995 (IBM PC and compatibles)

Learners' guide to the Internet
(CD-ROM for Mac and Windows), SCET, 1997

Your easy access to the Internet (CD-ROM),
CompuServe, 1995 (IBM PC and compatibles)

Service providers
There are currently over 250 Internet access providers. For up-to-date information, consult one of the Internet magazines or the URL:
http://www.limitless.co.uk/inetuk/providers.html.

The list below, which is not intended to be exhaustive, concentrates on service providers known to cater for the education sector.

AOL (America Online), Freepost LON616
London SW6 1YZ, Tel: 0800 279 1234
http://www.aol.com/

ArgoNet, 7 Dukes Court, Chichester, West Sussex
PO19 2FX, Tel: 01243 815 815 Fax: 01243 815 805
http://www.argonet.co.uk

BT CampusWorld, Westside, London Road,
Hemel Hempstead, Hertfordshire, HP3 9RR
Tel: 0345 626253 Fax: 01442 295273
http://www.campus.bt.com/CampusWorld

Demon Internet Ltd, Gateway House, 322 Regents
Park Road, Finchley, London N3 2QQ
Tel: 0181 371 1234 Fax: 0181 371 1150
http://www.demon.net

DIALnet, Western House, 43 Smallbrook, Queensway
Birmingham, B5 4HQ , Tel: 0121 624 5050
Fax: 0121 643 2448, http://www.dialnet.com/

The Education Exchange (Edex), 43 Wimbledon Hill
Road, Wimbledon, London SW19 7NA
Tel: 0181 296 9201 Fax: 0181 296 9282
http://www.edex.net.uk/

Internet for Learning (IFL), Research Machines,
New Mill House, 183 Milton Park, Abingdon
Oxford OX14 4SE, Tel: 01235 826000
Fax: 01235 826999, http://www.rmplc.net

Microsoft Network, Microsoft Place, Winnersh,
Wokingham, Berkshire RG41 5TP. Tel: 0345 002000
http://www.uk.msn.com/

VirginNet, PO Box 219, Newport NP1 9ZE
Tel: 0500 55 88 00 (subscriptions)
http://www.virgin.net/

Section 7

Glossary

The terminology used in **ICT** grows almost daily. Here is a list of some of the most common terms.

Bandwidth
This refers to the amount of traffic one cable can transfer simultaneously. For example, one strand of a broadband fibre-optic cable can carry over 30,000 telephone calls or hundreds of television channels simultaneously. A school would be able to connect to a telephone service, numerous television channels and on-line services through one broadband cable.

Browser
A program used to search and retrieve information from the World Wide Web

Bulletin Board
A single newsgroup

CMC
Computer Mediated Communication, the ability to send messages via a computer and a modem

Dial-up access
System by which users connect to the Internet over an ordinary telephone line by dialling up an Internet Service Provider's PoP

Electronic mail (e-mail)
The sending and receiving of messages via the Internet; anyone who subscribes to the Internet is given a unique address which enables users to send messages to, and receive messages from, any other user.

Filtered service
A service offered by ISPs through which access to the Internet is restricted, preventing access to sites known to contain offensive material

HTML
Hypertext Mark-up Language, a code which is used to indicate how information will be displayed on the World Wide Web. HTML files are read by a browser.

FTP (File Transfer Protocol)
This enables the transfer of a copy of a document from a remote computer to your computer

Gopher
A menu-based system for accessing and retrieving files